Simple Keto Instant Pot Cookbook

Healthy and Authentic Recipes With Stunning Photos

James A. Mabe

Introduction

Are you ready to embark on a culinary journey that combines the simplicity of keto cooking with the convenience of your Instant Pot? Look no further. James A. Mabe's Simple Keto Instant Pot Cookbook is your ultimate guide to effortlessly creating delicious, healthy, and authentic meals. Imagine transforming your kitchen into a haven of mouthwatering aromas and delectable dishes, all while staying true to your keto lifestyle.

Struggling to find keto recipes that are both easy and satisfying? This cookbook has you covered. Whether you're a seasoned keto enthusiast or just starting, you'll find a treasure trove of recipes that fit perfectly into your busy schedule.

Packed with stunning photos that make your mouth water, each recipe in this cookbook is crafted to provide you with the best keto experience. From hearty breakfasts to sumptuous dinners and everything in between, you'll discover a variety of dishes that are not only healthy but also incredibly flavorful. James A. Mabe has meticulously curated these recipes to ensure they are as simple as they are delicious, allowing you to enjoy the benefits of keto without the hassle.

Picture yourself savoring a creamy, rich keto cheesecake, or a perfectly cooked, tender beef stew made in your Instant Pot with minimal effort. These recipes are designed to save you time in the kitchen while delivering maximum taste and nutrition. Each dish is a testament to the power of keto cooking, proving that you don't have to sacrifice flavor for health.

Copyright

Copyright © 2024 by James A. Mabe.
All rights reserved. No part of this publication may be reproduced, distributed, or transmitted in any form or by any means, including photocopying, recording, or other electronic or mechanical methods, without the prior written permission of the publisher, except in the case of brief quotations embodied in critical reviews and specific other noncommercial uses permitted by copyright law. For permission requests, write to the publisher at the address below.
James A. Mabe

This book is a work of the author's research and experience. The recipes and nutritional information provided herein are based on the author's expertise and personal experience. The author and publisher are not responsible for any adverse effects or consequences arising from the use or misuse of the information contained in this book. Always consult with a healthcare professional before making any dietary or lifestyle changes, especially if you have any pre-existing health conditions or are taking any medications.

The information contained in this book is for informational purposes only. While the author has made every effort to ensure the accuracy and completeness of the information, the author assumes no responsibility for errors or omissions or any outcomes related to using this information. The reader should use this information at their own risk. The author and publisher disclaim any liability for any loss or damage caused directly or indirectly by the information contained in this book.

Contents

Chapter 1: Breakfasts 6
   Recipe 01: Omelet Muffin With Vegetables 6
   Recipe 02: Low Carb Cheese Pancakes 8
   Recipe 03: Blueberry Muffins 10
   Recipe 04: Egg Omelet With Tomatoes 12
   Recipe 05: Egg, Bacon, Vegetable Patties 14
   Recipe 06: Oatmeal Coconut Porridge 16
   Recipe 07: Salmon With Scrambled Eggs 18
   Recipe 08: Quinoa Porridge With Pumpkin 20
   Recipe 09: Fried Eggs With Chorizo 22
   Recipe 10: Fresh Baked Cinnamon Rolls 24

Chapter 2: Soups and Stews 26
   Recipe 11: Broccoli Cheddar Cheese Soup 26
   Recipe 12: Meat Potato Stew 28
   Recipe 13: Mexican Enchiladas 30
   Recipe 14: Roasted Pumpkin and Carrot Soup 32
   Recipe 15: Cauliflower Soup With Bacon 34
   Recipe 16: Beef Bone Broth 36
   Recipe 17: Kale Soup With Sausage 38
   Recipe 18: Turkey Meatbals Zoodle Soup 40
   Recipe 19: Soup Puree With Mushrooms 42
   Recipe 20: Tomato Soup With Fennel 44

Chapter 3: Main Dishes Beef 46
   Recipe 21: Sticky Beef Short Ribs 46
   Recipe 22: Beef Brisket Flat Steak 48
   Recipe 23: Swedish Meatballs 50
   Recipe 24: Beef Striploin Steak 52
   Recipe 25: Beef With Balsamic Vinegar 54
   Recipe 26: Beef Stroganoff With Mushrooms 56
   Recipe 27: Spicy Meat Beef Curry 58

Recipe 28: Beef Bourguignon...60

Recipe 29: Mexican Tacos With Meat 62

Recipe 30: Roasted Beef With Broccoli..64

Chapter 4: Main Dishes Poultry 66

Recipe 31: Butter Chicken Curry 66

Recipe 32: Green Chicken Curry 68

Recipe 33: Alfredo Pasta With Chicken 70

Recipe 34: Chicken Tikka With Rice..72

Recipe 35: Buffalo Wings With Dip..74

Recipe 36: Chili Chicken With Chives 76

Recipe 37: Chicken With Teriyaki Sauce 78

Recipe 38: Chicken With Potatoes 80

Recipe 39: Chicken Cacciatore 82

Recipe 40: Chicken With Mashed Potatoes 84

Chapter 5: Main Dishes Seafood..86

Recipe 41: Lobster Tails With Butter Sauce 86

Recipe 42: Shrimp Scampi With Garlic..88

Recipe 43: Salmon and Green Asparagus 90

Recipe 44: Tuna Steak Fish and Salad..92

Recipe 45: Cod With Beans and Potatoes 94

Recipe 46: Shrimp Gumbo Prawns...96

Recipe47: Coconut Curry With Shrimps 98

Recipe 48: Clam Chowder 100

Recipe 49: Mussels With Sauce..102

Recipe 50: Grilled Scallops Shell 104

Conclusion...106

Chapter 1: Breakfasts

Recipe 01: Omelet Muffin With Vegetables

Start your day with these delightful egg bites packed with vegetables and baked to perfection. These keto-friendly omelet muffins are a breeze to make using your Instant Pot, making them an ideal breakfast for those on a low-carb diet. They're not only delicious but also nutritious, ensuring you stay energized all morning long.

Servings: 4

Prepping Time: 10 minutes

Cook Time: 15 minutes

Difficulty: Easy

Ingredients:

- 6 large eggs
- 1/2 cup bell peppers, finely chopped
- 1/2 cup spinach, chopped
- 1/4 cup onions, finely chopped
- 1/4 cup shredded cheese
- 2 tablespoons heavy cream
- 1 tablespoon fresh herbs (e.g., parsley, chives), chopped
- Salt and pepper to taste
- Cooking spray

Step-by-Step Preparation:

1. Whisk eggs, heavy cream, salt, and pepper in a bowl until well combined.
2. Add bell peppers, spinach, onions, and shredded cheese to the egg mixture.
3. Grease silicone muffin molds with cooking spray and pour the mixture evenly into the molds.
4. Place the molds on the trivet in the Instant Pot with 1 cup of water.
5. Seal the lid, set it to manual high pressure for 8 minutes, and let it naturally release for 5 minutes.
6. Carefully remove the molds, let them cool slightly, and enjoy.

Nutritional Facts (Per serving)

- Calories: 120
- Fat: 8g
- Protein: 10g
- Fiber: 1g
- Carbohydrates: 3g

These egg bites are perfect for meal prep, allowing you to enjoy a quick and healthy breakfast throughout the week. Store them in the fridge, and reheat them for a delicious and convenient start to your day. Enjoy the balance of flavors and the ease of making this keto-friendly recipe.

Recipe 02: Low Carb Cheese Pancakes

If you're on a keto diet and craving something indulgent yet healthy, these low-carb cheese pancakes are perfect for a protein-packed breakfast. Made effortlessly in an Instant Pot, they offer a quick, delicious start to your day while keeping you on track with your carb goals.

Servings: 4

Prepping Time: 10 minutes

Cook Time: 20 minutes

Difficulty: Easy

Ingredients:

- ✓ 1 cup almond flour
- ✓ 1/2 cup cream cheese
- ✓ 4 large eggs
- ✓ 1 tsp vanilla extract
- ✓ 1 tbsp coconut oil
- ✓ 1/4 cup unsweetened almond milk
- ✓ 1 tsp baking powder
- ✓ Pinch of salt

Step-by-Step Preparation:

1. Combine almond flour, cream cheese, eggs, vanilla extract, and almond milk in a large bowl. Mix until smooth.
2. Add baking powder and salt, stirring to incorporate.
3. Set the Instant Pot to saute mode and heat the coconut oil.
4. Pour the batter into the pot, forming small pancakes.
5. Cook each pancake for 2-3 minutes per side until golden brown.
6. Serve warm with your favorite keto-friendly toppings.

Nutritional Facts: (Per serving)

- ❖ **Calories:** 150
- ❖ **Carbohydrates:** 4g
- ❖ **Protein:** 8g
- ❖ **Fiber:** 2g
- ❖ **Fat:** 12g

Enjoy your keto journey with these delicious cheese pancakes. Perfect for a quick breakfast or a tasty snack, they'll keep you satisfied and energized throughout your day.

Recipe 03: Blueberry Muffins

Start your day with these delicious Keto Blueberry Muffins, made effortlessly in the Instant Pot. They're the perfect low-carb breakfast treat, with juicy blueberries and a hint of vanilla. Enjoy the warm, fluffy texture that melts in your mouth, making your mornings brighter and healthier.

Servings: 6 muffins

Cook Time: 20 minutes

Prepping Time: 10 minutes

Difficulty: Easy

Ingredients:

- ✓ 1 cup almond flour
- ✓ 2 tbsp coconut flour
- ✓ 1/4 cup erythritol
- ✓ 1 tsp baking powder
- ✓ 1/4 tsp salt
- ✓ 3 large eggs
- ✓ 1/4 cup unsweetened almond milk
- ✓ 1/4 cup melted coconut oil
- ✓ 1 tsp vanilla extract
- ✓ 1/2 cup fresh blueberries

Step-by-Step Preparation:

1. Whisk together almond flour, coconut flour, erythritol, baking powder, and salt in a large bowl.
2. In another bowl, beat the eggs, then add almond milk, melted coconut oil, and vanilla extract.
3. Combine wet and dry ingredients, mixing until just combined.
4. Fold in the blueberries gently.
5. Pour the batter into silicone muffin cups, filling each about two-thirds full.
6. Place the muffin cups in the Instant Pot on a trivet with 1 cup of water at the bottom.
7. Seal the lid and cook on high pressure for 20 minutes.
8. Allow natural pressure for 5 minutes, then quickly release the remaining pressure.
9. Carefully remove the muffins and let them cool before serving.

Nutritional Facts: (Per serving)

- ❖ Calories: 150
- ❖ Fat: 12g
- ❖ Carbohydrates: 6g
- ❖ Fiber: 3g
- ❖ Protein: 4g
- ❖ Sugar: 2g

Enjoy these delightful keto blueberry muffins as a quick breakfast or a tasty snack. Their convenience and health benefits make them a fantastic addition to your keto diet, giving you a burst of energy to start your day. Perfectly portioned and easy to prepare, these muffins will become a favorite in your household.

Recipe 04: Egg Omelet With Tomatoes

Start your day with a delicious and nutritious Keto Frittata packed with fresh herbs, juicy tomatoes, and creamy feta cheese. This Instant Pot recipe is perfect for a quick, healthy breakfast that will energize and satisfy all morning.

Servings: 4

Cook Time: 20 minutes

Prepping Time: 10 minutes

Difficulty: Easy

Ingredients:
- ✓ 8 large eggs
- ✓ 1/4 cup heavy cream
- ✓ 1/2 cup crumbled feta cheese
- ✓ 1 cup cherry tomatoes, halved
- ✓ 1/4 cup chopped fresh herbs (parsley, basil, or chives)
- ✓ Salt and pepper to taste
- ✓ 2 tablespoons olive oil

Step-by-Step Preparation:
1. Whisk the eggs and heavy cream in a bowl. Season with salt and pepper.
2. Stir in the crumbled feta cheese, cherry tomatoes, and chopped herbs.
3. Set the Instant Pot to saute mode and add olive oil.
4. Pour the egg mixture into the Instant Pot and cook for 5 minutes.
5. Switch to the pressure cook setting for 15 minutes on low pressure.
6. Let the pressure release naturally for 5 minutes before opening.
7. Slice and serve hot.

Nutritional Facts: (Per serving)
- ❖ Calories: 250
- ❖ Fat: 20g
- ❖ Protein: 15g
- ❖ Carbs: 5g

Enjoy your Keto Frittata as a flavorful and satisfying start to your day. It's perfect for meal prep and can be enjoyed warm or cold. This recipe is easy to make and versatile, allowing you to customize it with your favorite herbs and vegetables.

Recipe 05: Egg, Bacon, Vegetable Patties

This keto-friendly Instant Pot breakfast is a delicious and hearty start to your day, featuring a perfectly fried egg, crispy bacon, flavorful vegetable patties, creamy avocado, and a zesty tomato relish. It's a quick and nutritious option for those following a low-carb diet, ensuring you stay energized and satisfied throughout your morning.

Servings: 4

Prepping Time: 15 minutes

Cook Time: 10 minutes

Difficulty: Medium

Ingredients:

- ✓ 4 eggs
- ✓ 8 slices of bacon
- ✓ 2 cups shredded zucchini
- ✓ 1 cup grated carrots
- ✓ 1 avocado, sliced
- ✓ 1 cup cherry tomatoes, chopped
- ✓ 1 tablespoon olive oil
- ✓ 1 teaspoon lemon juice
- ✓ Salt and pepper to taste

Step-by-Step Preparation:

1. **Prepare the Vegetable Patties:**
    - ➢ Mix shredded zucchini, grated carrots, salt, and pepper in a bowl.
    - ➢ Form small patties and set aside.
2. **Cook the Bacon:**
    - ➢ Set the Instant Pot to saute mode.
    - ➢ Cook the bacon until crispy, then remove and set aside.
3. **Cook the Patties:**
    - ➢ In the same Instant Pot, cook the vegetable patties until golden brown on both sides. Remove and set aside.
4. **Fry the Eggs:**
    - ➢ Add some oil if needed, then fry the eggs to your preferred doneness.
5. **Prepare the Tomato Relish:**
    - ➢ Mix chopped cherry tomatoes, olive oil, lemon juice, salt, and pepper in a bowl.
6. **Assemble the Dish:**
    - ➢ Place the patties on a plate and top with fried egg, bacon, avocado slices, and spoonfuls of tomato relish.

Nutritional Facts (Per serving)

- ❖ Calories: 350
- ❖ Protein: 15g
- ❖ Fat: 28g
- ❖ Carbohydrates: 7g
- ❖ Fiber: 4g

Enjoy this vibrant and satisfying keto breakfast that combines savory flavors and healthy ingredients. Whether you're starting your day at home or on the go, this dish is perfect for keeping you full and energized while staying on track with your low-carb lifestyle.

Recipe 06: Oatmeal Coconut Porridge

Start your day with a hearty and delicious Keto Instant Pot breakfast recipe that combines the creamy texture of oatmeal with the tropical flavor of coconut. Topped with fresh blueberries and crunchy almonds, this easy-to-make porridge will keep you energized and satisfied throughout the morning.

Servings: 4

Prepping Time: 10 minutes

Cook Time: 5 minutes

Difficulty: Easy

Ingredients:

- ✓ 1 cup unsweetened shredded coconut
- ✓ 2 cups unsweetened almond milk
- ✓ 1/4 cup chia seeds
- ✓ 1/4 cup hemp seeds
- ✓ 1/4 cup unsweetened coconut flakes
- ✓ 1/4 cup sliced almonds
- ✓ 1/2 cup fresh blueberries
- ✓ 2 tbsp erythritol or keto-friendly sweetener
- ✓ 1 tsp vanilla extract
- ✓ 1/2 tsp ground cinnamon
- ✓ Pinch of salt

Step-by-Step Preparation:

1. Add almond milk, shredded coconut, chia seeds, hemp seeds, coconut flakes, erythritol, vanilla extract, cinnamon, and salt into the Instant Pot.
2. Stir the mixture until well combined.
3. Secure the lid and set the Instant Pot to "Porridge" for 5 minutes.
4. Once the cooking time is complete, allow the pressure to release naturally.
5. Open the lid and stir the porridge.
6. Divide the porridge into bowls and top with sliced almonds and fresh blueberries.
7. Serve warm and enjoy.

Nutritional Facts (Per serving)

- ❖ Calories: 220
- ❖ Protein: 6g
- ❖ Fat: 18g
- ❖ Carbohydrates: 9g
- ❖ Fiber: 7g
- ❖ Sugar: 2g

This oatmeal coconut porridge with blueberries and almonds is a perfect keto-friendly breakfast that is both nutritious and satisfying. Combining creamy coconut and crunchy almonds with the burst of blueberry flavor makes every bite delightful. Enjoy this quick and easy recipe that fits perfectly into your keto lifestyle.

Recipe 07: Salmon With Scrambled Eggs

Indulge in a luxurious Keto breakfast with our Smoked Salmon with Dill Cream, Capers, and Scrambled Eggs. This Instant Pot recipe combines rich, smoky flavors with creamy, tangy dill and perfectly scrambled eggs for a delightful start to your day.

Servings: 2

Prepping Time: 10 minutes

Cook Time: 10 minutes

Difficulty: Easy

Ingredients:
- ✓ 4 large eggs
- ✓ 2 oz smoked salmon, thinly sliced
- ✓ 1/4 cup heavy cream
- ✓ 1 tbsp fresh dill, chopped
- ✓ 1 tbsp capers, drained
- ✓ Salt and pepper to taste
- ✓ 1 tbsp butter

Step-by-Step Preparation:
1. Whisk together the eggs, heavy cream, salt, and pepper in a bowl.
2. Set the Instant Pot to saute mode and melt the butter.
3. Pour the egg mixture into the Instant Pot and stir gently until they set.
4. Add the smoked salmon, dill, and capers, and cook until the eggs are fully set.
5. Serve immediately with an extra sprinkle of dill for garnish.

Nutritional Facts: (Per serving)
- ✓ Calories: 250
- ✓ Fat: 20g
- ✓ Protein: 18g
- ✓ Carbohydrates: 2g

This delectable breakfast recipe is perfect for those following a Keto diet. It's quick, easy, and flavorful, making it a great way to start your day. Enjoy the blend of creamy eggs, smoky salmon, and fresh dill, and savor the simplicity of this Instant Pot delight.

Recipe 08: Quinoa Porridge With Pumpkin

Start your day with a warm, comforting bowl of tasty quinoa porridge with pumpkin. This keto-friendly recipe is perfect for a quick and nutritious breakfast. Combining quinoa and pumpkin creates a creamy texture, while the Instant Pot makes it a breeze to prepare. Enjoy this delicious dish that's packed with flavor and health benefits.

Servings: 4

Prepping Time: 10 minutes

Cook Time: 20 minutes

Difficulty: Easy

Ingredients:

- ✓ 1 cup quinoa, rinsed
- ✓ 1 cup pumpkin puree
- ✓ 2 cups unsweetened almond milk
- ✓ 1 cup water
- ✓ 1 tsp cinnamon
- ✓ 1/2 tsp nutmeg
- ✓ 1/4 tsp cloves
- ✓ 1/4 tsp salt
- ✓ 1 tsp vanilla extract
- ✓ Stevia or keto-friendly sweetener, to taste
- ✓ Optional toppings: nuts, seeds, coconut flakes

Step-by-Step Preparation:

1. Add quinoa, pumpkin puree, almond milk, water, cinnamon, nutmeg, cloves, and salt to the Instant Pot.
2. Stir well to combine all ingredients.
3. Secure the lid and set the Instant Pot to high pressure for 5 minutes.
4. Once the cooking cycle is complete, allow the pressure to release naturally for 10 minutes, then quickly release any remaining pressure.
5. Open the lid and stir in the vanilla extract and sweetener.
6. Serve the porridge in bowls and add your favorite toppings.

Nutritional Facts: (Per serving)

- ❖ Calories: 150
- ❖ Protein: 5g
- ❖ Carbohydrates: 25g
- ❖ Fat: 3g
- ❖ Fiber: 4g

Enjoy the rich and creamy flavors of this quinoa porridge with pumpkin. It's a delightful way to start your morning, offering a perfect balance of taste and nutrition. Whether following a keto diet or just looking for a healthy breakfast option, this recipe will satisfy you. Enjoy every spoonful.

Recipe 09: Fried Eggs With Chorizo

Start your day with a flavorful punch by making Fried Eggs with Chorizo, a perfect Keto Instant Pot breakfast. This easy recipe combines the rich taste of chorizo with the simplicity of fried eggs, creating a hearty and delicious meal that's low in carbs and high in protein.

Servings: 2

Prepping Time: 5 minutes

Cook Time: 10 minutes

Difficulty: Easy

Ingredients:

- 4 large eggs
- 100g chorizo, sliced
- 1 tbsp olive oil
- Salt and pepper to taste
- Fresh parsley, chopped (optional)

Step-by-Step Preparation:

1. Heat the Instant Pot on saute mode and add olive oil.
2. Add sliced chorizo and cook for 2-3 minutes until slightly crispy.
3. Push the chorizo to the side and crack the eggs into the pot.
4. Season with salt and pepper.
5. Cook until the egg whites are set, but the yolks remain runny for 3-4 minutes.
6. Serve hot, garnished with chopped parsley if desired.

Nutritional Facts (Per serving)

- Calories: 280
- Protein: 18g
- Fat: 22g
- Carbs: 1g

Enjoy this quick and satisfying Keto breakfast, which is sure to keep you full and energized throughout the morning. The combination of fried eggs and spicy chorizo will make your taste buds dance, and the Instant Pot makes it a breeze to prepare. Happy cooking.

Recipe 10: Fresh Baked Cinnamon Rolls

There's nothing better than waking up to the warm, inviting aroma of fresh-baked cinnamon rolls. This keto-friendly recipe uses an Instant Pot for a quick and easy breakfast treat that's low in carbs but high in flavor. These cinnamon rolls are perfect for any morning and will delight your taste buds without compromising your diet.

Servings: 8

Cook Time: 25 minutes

Prepping Time: 15 minutes

Difficulty: Moderate

Ingredients:

- ✓ 2 cups almond flour
- ✓ 1/2 cup coconut flour
- ✓ 1/4 cup erythritol
- ✓ 2 tsp baking powder
- ✓ 1/2 tsp salt
- ✓ 1/2 cup unsweetened almond milk
- ✓ 2 large eggs
- ✓ 1/4 cup melted butter
- ✓ 2 tsp vanilla extract
- ✓ 2 tbsp cinnamon
- ✓ 1/4 cup cream cheese
- ✓ 1/4 cup powdered erythritol
- ✓ 1 tsp vanilla extract

Step-by-Step Preparation:

1. Mix almond flour, coconut flour, erythritol, baking powder, and salt in a large bowl.
2. Whisk together almond milk, eggs, melted butter, and vanilla extract in another bowl.
3. Combine the wet and dry ingredients, stirring until a dough forms.
4. Roll out the dough between two sheets of parchment paper.
5. Spread the cream cheese over the dough and sprinkle with cinnamon and powdered erythritol.
6. Roll up the dough into a log and cut into 8 equal slices.
7. Place the rolls in a greased Instant Pot, set to high pressure for 15 minutes, and allow natural release.
8. Mix cream cheese, powdered erythritol, and vanilla extract to prepare the icing. Drizzle over warm rolls.

Nutritional Facts: (Per serving)

- ❖ Calories: 210
- ❖ Total Fat: 18g
- ❖ Saturated Fat: 6g
- ❖ Cholesterol: 50mg
- ❖ Sodium: 190mg
- ❖ Total Carbohydrate: 6g
- ❖ Dietary Fiber: 3g
- ❖ Sugars: 1g
- ❖ Protein: 6g

Enjoy these delicious keto cinnamon rolls as a perfect start to your day. Whether on a ketogenic diet or just looking for a healthier breakfast option, this recipe will satisfy your cravings while keeping you on track with your goals. Enjoy every bite.

Chapter 2: Soups and Stews

Recipe 11: Broccoli Cheddar Cheese Soup

Craving a hearty, keto-friendly meal? This Broccoli Cheddar Cheese Soup is a comforting classic made quick and easy in your Instant Pot. Packed with flavor and low in carbs, it's perfect for those chilly days when you need a warm, satisfying bowl of soup.

Servings: 4

Cook Time: 20 minutes

Prepping Time: 10 minutes

Difficulty: Easy

Ingredients:

- ✓ 4 cups broccoli florets
- ✓ 1 cup shredded cheddar cheese
- ✓ 1 cup heavy cream
- ✓ 2 cups chicken broth
- ✓ 1 small onion, diced
- ✓ 2 cloves garlic, minced
- ✓ 2 tbsp butter
- ✓ Salt and pepper to taste

Step-by-Step Preparation:

1. Set the Instant Pot to saute and melt the butter.
2. Add the diced onion and minced garlic and saute until fragrant.
3. Add the broccoli florets and chicken broth, then close the lid and set the Instant Pot to manual high pressure for 5 minutes.
4. Quickly release the pressure and open the lid.
5. Stir in the heavy cream and shredded cheddar cheese until melted and combined.
6. Use an immersion blender to blend the soup to your desired consistency.
7. Season with salt and pepper to taste.

Nutritional Facts: (Per serving)

- ❖ Calories: 250
- ❖ Fat: 20g
- ❖ Carbohydrates: 6g
- ❖ Protein: 10g

Enjoy a bowl of this creamy Broccoli Cheddar Cheese Soup, perfect for a quick lunch or dinner. It's delicious and keeps you on track with your keto goals. Try this recipe today and savor the comfort of homemade soup made effortlessly in your Instant Pot.

Recipe 12: Meat Potato Stew

Hearty and satisfying, this Keto Instant Pot Meat Potato Stew is perfect for a comforting meal. This stew is rich in flavor and nutrition and combines tender meat with low-carb potatoes. Easy to prepare and perfect for a cozy dinner, it's a must-try for those following a keto lifestyle.

Servings: 4

Prepping Time: 15 minutes

Cook Time: 35 minutes

Difficulty: Easy

Ingredients:

- ✓ 1 lb beef stew meat, cubed
- ✓ 2 cups low-carb potatoes, diced
- ✓ 1 onion, chopped
- ✓ 3 cloves garlic, minced
- ✓ 4 cups beef broth
- ✓ 2 tbsp olive oil
- ✓ 1 tsp thyme
- ✓ 1 tsp rosemary
- ✓ Salt and pepper to taste

Step-by-Step Preparation:

1. Set the Instant Pot to saute mode and heat the olive oil.
2. Add the beef and brown on all sides.
3. Add the onion and garlic, sauteing until softened.
4. Add the low-carb potatoes, beef broth, thyme, rosemary, salt, and pepper.
5. Seal the Instant Pot and set it to pressure cook on high for 35 minutes.
6. Allow the pressure to release naturally for 10 minutes, then quickly release any remaining pressure.
7. Stir the stew and serve hot.

Nutritional Facts: (Per serving)

- ❖ Calories: 320
- ❖ Protein: 25g
- ❖ Fat: 20g
- ❖ Carbohydrates: 8g
- ❖ Fiber: 2g
- ❖ Net Carbs: 6g

This Keto Instant Pot Meat Potato Stew delivers on taste and nutrition, perfect for a busy weeknight or a weekend gathering. Enjoy the rich, savory flavors while staying true to your keto diet. Bon appetit.

Recipe 13: Mexican Enchiladas

Craving a taste of Mexico while staying true to your keto diet? This Keto Mexican Enchilada recipe is a perfect blend of rich flavors and healthy ingredients, made effortlessly in your Instant Pot. Ideal for any meal, it's sure to become a household favorite.

Servings: 4

Prepping Time: 15 minutes

Cook Time: 35 minutes

Difficulty: Medium

Ingredients:

- ✓ 1 lb ground beef
- ✓ 1 cup chopped onions
- ✓ 2 cloves garlic, minced
- ✓ 1 cup bell peppers, diced
- ✓ 1 cup enchilada sauce (sugar-free)
- ✓ 1 cup shredded cheddar cheese
- ✓ 2 cups cauliflower rice
- ✓ 1 tbsp olive oil
- ✓ 1 tsp chili powder
- ✓ 1 tsp cumin
- ✓ Salt and pepper to taste

Step-by-Step Preparation:

1. Set your Instant Pot to saute mode and add olive oil.
2. Add ground beef, onions, and garlic. Cook until meat is browned.
3. Add bell peppers, enchilada sauce, chili powder, cumin, salt, and pepper. Stir well.
4. Switch to pressure cook mode and set for 15 minutes.
5. Release pressure naturally, then stir in cauliflower rice and half the cheese.
6. Top with remaining cheese, close the lid and let it melt for 5 minutes.
7. Serve hot and enjoy.

Nutritional Facts: (Per serving)

- ❖ Calories: 300
- ❖ Protein: 25g
- ❖ Fat: 20g
- ❖ Carbohydrates: 8g
- ❖ Fiber: 4g

Delight in every bite of these savory, keto-friendly enchiladas. They're a surefire way to bring authentic Mexican cuisine to your table while keeping your diet goals on track. Perfect for busy weeknights or a cozy weekend meal, this dish is as simple as it is delicious. Enjoy the vibrant flavors and nutritious benefits.

Recipe 14: Roasted Pumpkin and Carrot Soup

There's nothing more comforting than a warm bowl of Roasted Pumpkin and Carrot Soup with Cream and Pumpkin Seeds. This keto-friendly recipe is perfect for those chilly days when you crave something hearty yet healthy. Made in an Instant Pot, it's quick and easy to prepare, ensuring you spend less time in the kitchen and more time enjoying your meal.

Servings: 4

Prepping Time: 10 minutes

Cook Time: 20 minutes

Difficulty: Easy

Ingredients:

- ✓ 2 cups pumpkin, peeled and diced
- ✓ 2 cups carrots, peeled and diced
- ✓ 1 medium onion, chopped
- ✓ 2 cloves garlic, minced
- ✓ 4 cups chicken or vegetable broth
- ✓ 1 cup heavy cream
- ✓ 2 tbsp olive oil
- ✓ 1 tsp ground cumin
- ✓ 1 tsp smoked paprika
- ✓ Salt and pepper to taste
- ✓ 1/4 cup pumpkin seeds, toasted

Step-by-Step Preparation:

1. Set the Instant Pot to saute mode and add olive oil.
2. Add onions and garlic, and saute until translucent.
3. Add pumpkin, carrots, cumin, paprika, salt, and pepper. Stir well.
4. Pour in the broth and close the lid. Set to high pressure for 15 minutes.
5. Once done, allow natural release for 10 minutes, then manually release any remaining pressure.
6. Use an immersion blender to blend until smooth.
7. Stir in the heavy cream.
8. Ladle the soup into bowls and top with toasted pumpkin seeds.

Nutritional Facts: (Per serving)

- ❖ Calories: 250
- ❖ Total Fat: 20g
- ❖ Carbohydrates: 10g
- ❖ Protein: 5g
- ❖ Fiber: 4g

Enjoy this flavorful and creamy roasted pumpkin and carrot soup as a perfect meal for any occasion. Rich cream and crunchy pumpkin seeds add a delightful texture, satisfying every spoonful. Ideal for those following a keto diet, this soup is both nutritious and delicious.

Recipe 15: Cauliflower Soup With Bacon

Cauliflower Cream Soup with Bacon and Gorgonzola is a comforting, keto-friendly delight perfect for a cozy dinner. The combination of creamy cauliflower, crispy bacon, and tangy Gorgonzola makes this soup a delicious and satisfying meal that's easy to prepare in your Instant Pot.

Servings: 4

Prepping Time: 10 minutes

Cook Time: 20 minutes

Difficulty: Easy

Ingredients:

- 1 head of cauliflower, chopped
- 4 slices of bacon, chopped
- 1/2 cup Gorgonzola cheese, crumbled
- 1 small onion, diced
- 2 cloves garlic, minced
- 4 cups chicken broth
- 1 cup heavy cream
- Salt and pepper to taste
- Fresh parsley for garnish (optional)

Step-by-Step Preparation:

1. Set the Instant Pot to saute mode. Cook the bacon until crispy, then remove and set aside.
2. Add the onion and garlic to the pot, sautéing until translucent.
3. Add the chopped cauliflower and chicken broth. Close the lid and set it to high pressure for 8 minutes.
4. Quickly release the pressure. Use an immersion blender to puree the soup until smooth.
5. Stir in the heavy cream and Gorgonzola cheese until well combined.
6. Season with salt and pepper to taste.
7. Serve hot, garnished with crispy bacon and fresh parsley.

Nutritional Facts (Per serving)

- Calories: 320
- Fat: 25g
- Protein: 12g
- Carbohydrates: 8g
- Fiber: 3g

Enjoy this rich and hearty Cauliflower Cream Soup with Bacon and Gorgonzola, a perfect addition to your keto meal plan. It's a simple yet flavorful recipe that brings gourmet quality to your home kitchen, making weeknight dinners easy and delightful.

Recipe 16: Beef Bone Broth

Experience the rich, nourishing flavors of Beef Bone Broth with this Keto Instant Pot recipe. This broth is a powerhouse of nutrients, perfect for soups and stews, making it an excellent addition to your keto diet. With minimal prepping and cooking time, you'll have a delicious broth ready to enhance your meals.

Servings: 6

Cook Time: 2 hours

Prepping Time: 10 minutes

Difficulty: Easy

Ingredients:

- 2 lbs beef bones (preferably with marrow)
- 1 onion, quartered
- 2 carrots, chopped
- 2 celery stalks, chopped
- 4 garlic cloves, smashed
- 2 tbsp apple cider vinegar
- 1 tsp salt
- 1 tsp black peppercorns
- 2 bay leaves
- 8 cups water

Step-by-Step Preparation:

1. Place the beef bones in the Instant Pot and add the onion, carrots, celery, and garlic.
2. Pour in the apple cider vinegar and season with salt, peppercorns, and bay leaves.
3. Add water, ensuring it covers the bones and vegetables.
4. Seal the Instant Pot and set it to high pressure for 2 hours.
5. Allow natural release for 30 minutes, then manually release any remaining pressure.
6. Strain the broth, discarding the solids. Store the broth in the refrigerator or freeze it for later use.

Nutritional Facts (Per serving)

- Calories: 80
- Protein: 6g
- Fat: 6g
- Carbohydrates: 2g
- Fiber: 1g
- Sodium: 300mg

Indulge in the comforting and healing benefits of this homemade Beef Bone Broth. Whether enjoyed on its own or as a base for other dishes, this nutrient-dense broth is a perfect addition to your keto lifestyle. Happy cooking.

Recipe 17: Kale Soup With Sausage

Warm up with a comforting bowl of Rustic Kale Soup with Sausage, a hearty keto recipe perfect for cozy nights. This Instant Pot delight combines savory sausage and nutrient-packed kale in a rich broth, making it an ideal meal for those on a low-carb diet.

Servings: 4

Prepping Time: 10 minutes

Cook Time: 20 minutes

Difficulty: Easy

Ingredients:

- ✓ 1 lb Italian sausage, sliced
- ✓ 1 bunch kale, chopped
- ✓ 1 medium onion, diced
- ✓ 3 cloves garlic, minced
- ✓ 4 cups chicken broth
- ✓ 1 cup heavy cream
- ✓ 1 tbsp olive oil
- ✓ Salt and pepper to taste

Step-by-Step Preparation:

1. Saute the Sausage: Set the Instant Pot to saute mode, add olive oil, and cook the sausage until browned.
2. Add Aromatics: Stir in onion and garlic, cooking until softened.
3. Combine Ingredients: Add kale, chicken broth, and heavy cream. Season with salt and pepper.
4. Pressure Cook: Secure the lid and set the pressure cooker on high for 5 minutes.
5. Release Pressure: Carefully release the pressure manually and stir the soup before serving.

Nutritional Facts (Per serving)

- ❖ Calories: 320
- ❖ Protein: 15g
- ❖ Fat: 27g
- ❖ Carbohydrates: 6g
- ❖ Fiber: 2g

Savor the rich flavors of this Rustic Kale Soup with Sausage, a quick and easy recipe that satisfies your cravings while keeping you on track with your keto goals. This dish will become a favorite in your meal rotation, perfect for busy weeknights. Enjoy every comforting spoonful.

Recipe 18: Turkey Meatbals Zoodle Soup

Turkey Meatball Zoodle Soup is a delicious, keto-friendly dish for any meal. This hearty soup combines tender turkey meatballs with fresh zucchini noodles, which are both flavorful and healthy. Made in an Instant Pot, it's quick and easy to prepare, making it an excellent option for busy days.

Servings: 4

Prepping Time: 15 minutes

Cook Time: 20 minutes

Difficulty: Easy

Ingredients:

- ✓ 1 lb ground turkey
- ✓ 1 large egg
- ✓ 1/4 cup grated Parmesan cheese
- ✓ 1/4 cup almond flour
- ✓ 2 cloves garlic, minced
- ✓ 1 tsp Italian seasoning
- ✓ Salt and pepper to taste
- ✓ 2 tbsp olive oil
- ✓ 4 cups chicken broth
- ✓ 2 medium zucchini, spiralized
- ✓ 1 cup spinach
- ✓ 1/2 cup diced tomatoes
- ✓ 1/2 cup diced onions
- ✓ 1/2 tsp red pepper flakes (optional)

Step-by-Step Preparation:

1. Combine ground turkey, egg, Parmesan cheese, almond flour, garlic, Italian seasoning, salt, and pepper in a bowl. Mix well and form into small meatballs.
2. Set the Instant Pot to saute mode, add olive oil, and brown the meatballs in batches. Remove and set aside.
3. Add onions to the pot and saute until translucent. Add chicken broth, diced tomatoes, and red pepper flakes.
4. Return the meatballs to the pot, close the lid, and set the pressure to cook on high for 10 minutes.
5. Once done, quickly release the pressure and add spiralized zucchini and spinach. Stir and let sit for a few minutes until the zucchini is tender.
6. Serve hot and enjoy.

Nutritional Facts: (Per serving)

- ❖ Calories: 250
- ❖ Protein: 25g
- ❖ Fat: 15g
- ❖ Carbohydrates: 6g
- ❖ Fiber: 2g
- ❖ Net Carbs: 4g

This Turkey Meatball Zoodle Soup is a satisfying and nutritious option for those following a keto diet. The combination of flavors and textures makes it a family favorite, perfect for any time of the year. Enjoy this quick and easy recipe that fits your dietary needs and delights your taste buds.

Recipe 19: Soup Puree With Mushrooms

Experience the rich and earthy flavors of our Keto Instant Pot Wild Mushroom Soup Puree. This deliciously creamy soup is perfect for those chilly days when you crave something warm and comforting. With a blend of wild mushrooms and aromatic herbs, this recipe is satisfying and keto-friendly, making it an ideal addition to your healthy meal repertoire.

Servings: 4

Cook Time: 25 minutes

Prepping Time: 15 minutes

Difficulty: Easy

Ingredients:

- ✓ 1 lb wild mushrooms, cleaned and chopped
- ✓ 1 small onion, diced
- ✓ 2 cloves garlic, minced
- ✓ 4 cups chicken or vegetable broth
- ✓ 1 cup heavy cream
- ✓ 2 tbsp olive oil
- ✓ 1 tsp thyme
- ✓ Salt and pepper to taste

Step-by-Step Preparation:

1. Set your Instant Pot to saute mode and heat the olive oil.
2. Add the onions and garlic, sauteing until fragrant and translucent.
3. Add the wild mushrooms and thyme, cooking until the mushrooms soften.
4. Pour the broth, seal the Instant Pot lid, and cook on high pressure for 10 minutes.
5. Release the pressure, then blend the mixture until smooth using an immersion blender.
6. Stir in the heavy cream, seasoning with salt and pepper to taste.
7. Serve hot, garnished with extra thyme if desired.

Nutritional Facts: (Per serving)

- ❖ Calories: 220
- ❖ Fat: 18g
- ❖ Protein: 5g
- ❖ Carbohydrates: 8g
- ❖ Fiber: 2g

Elevate your keto dining experience with this delectable Soup Puree with Wild Mushrooms. The Instant Pot ensures a quick and easy preparation, while the wild mushrooms provide a sophisticated touch. Enjoy this nourishing and satisfying soup, perfect for cozy evenings or impressing guests with minimal effort.

Recipe 20: Tomato Soup With Fennel

Looking for a delicious and keto-friendly soup? This Creamy Tomato Soup with Fennel Leaves is perfect for you. Made in an Instant Pot, it's quick, easy, and flavorful. Enjoy a warm bowl of this nutritious soup that satisfies your taste buds and aligns with your keto lifestyle.

Servings: 4

Prepping Time: 10 minutes

Cook Time: 20 minutes

Difficulty: Easy

Ingredients:
- 4 large tomatoes, chopped
- 1 fennel bulb, thinly sliced
- 2 cups chicken broth
- 1 cup heavy cream
- 2 cloves garlic, minced
- 1 tbsp olive oil
- Salt and pepper to taste
- Fresh fennel leaves for garnish

Step-by-Step Preparation:
1. Turn on the Instant Pot to saute mode and heat olive oil.
2. Add garlic and fennel bulb, and saute until fragrant.
3. Add chopped tomatoes and chicken broth, then season with salt and pepper.
4. Seal the Instant Pot lid and set to high pressure for 15 minutes.
5. Release pressure manually, then blend the soup until smooth.
6. Stir in heavy cream and garnish with fresh fennel leaves before serving.

Nutritional Facts (Per serving)
- Calories: 220
- Protein: 4g
- Fat: 18g
- Carbohydrates: 8g
- Fiber: 2g

Enjoy your creamy tomato soup with fennel leaves as a comforting and healthy keto meal. It's perfect for any occasion, offering a blend of rich flavors and smooth texture. Whether on a keto diet or simply craving a delicious soup, this recipe will become a favorite in your kitchen.

Chapter 3: Main Dishes Beef

Recipe 21: Sticky Beef Short Ribs

Looking for a mouth-watering, keto-friendly beef recipe that's perfect for your Instant Pot? These sticky beef short ribs are a delicious main dish that will impress. With an ideal balance of savory and sweet, this dish is tender, flavorful, and incredibly easy to make. Get ready to enjoy a restaurant-quality meal right at home.

Servings: 4

Prepping Time: 10 minutes

Cook Time: 1 hour

Difficulty: Medium

Ingredients:

- 2 lbs beef short ribs
- 1/4 cup soy sauce (or coconut aminos for keto)
- 1/4 cup beef broth
- 2 tbsp keto-friendly sweetener
- 2 cloves garlic, minced
- 1 tbsp fresh ginger, grated
- 1 tsp sesame oil
- 1 tbsp apple cider vinegar
- 1/4 tsp black pepper
- 1 tbsp sesame seeds (for garnish)
- 2 green onions, sliced (for garnish)

Step-by-Step Preparation:

1. Season the short ribs with salt and pepper.
2. Select the saute function on the Instant Pot and add sesame oil.
3. Brown the short ribs on all sides, then remove and set aside.
4. Add garlic and ginger to the pot and saute for 1 minute.
5. Pour in soy sauce, beef broth, sweetener, and apple cider vinegar. Stir well.
6. Return the short ribs to the pot, ensuring they are well-coated with the sauce.
7. Secure the lid, select the Meat/Stew setting, and set the timer for 45 minutes.
8. Once done, allow the pressure to release naturally for 10 minutes, then quickly release.
9. Remove the ribs and set aside. Switch to the saute function to reduce the sauce until thickened.
10. Serve the ribs with the sticky sauce, garnished with sesame seeds and green onions.

Nutritional Facts: (Per serving)

- Calories: 400
- Protein: 25g
- Fat: 30g
- Carbohydrates: 5g
- Fiber: 1g

These sticky beef short ribs are keto-friendly, incredibly satisfying, and easy to prepare. Enjoy a gourmet meal that fits perfectly into your low-carb lifestyle. Happy cooking and savor every bite.

Recipe 22: Beef Brisket Flat Steak

Get ready to indulge in a mouthwatering Keto-friendly roasted beef brisket flat steak. This Instant Pot recipe promises tender, juicy beef infused with rich flavors, perfect for a satisfying main dish. Whether hosting a dinner party or craving a hearty meal, this dish will be a crowd-pleaser.

Servings: 6

Prepping Time: 15 minutes

Cook Time: 1 hour 30 minutes

Difficulty: Moderate

Ingredients:

- ✓ 2 lbs beef brisket flat steak
- ✓ 2 tbsp olive oil
- ✓ 1 large onion, sliced
- ✓ 4 garlic cloves, minced
- ✓ 1 cup beef broth
- ✓ 2 tbsp tomato paste
- ✓ 1 tsp smoked paprika
- ✓ 1 tsp dried thyme
- ✓ Salt and pepper to taste

Step-by-Step Preparation:

1. Set the Instant Pot to saute mode and heat the olive oil.
2. Season the brisket with salt, pepper, smoked paprika, and thyme.
3. Sear the brisket on all sides until browned, then remove from the pot.
4. Add onion and garlic to the pot and saute until softened.
5. Stir in tomato paste and beef broth, scraping any browned bits from the bottom.
6. Return the brisket to the pot, secure the lid, and set it to high pressure for 90 minutes.
7. Once cooked, let the pressure release naturally for 10 minutes, then quickly release.
8. Remove the brisket, rest for 10 minutes, then slice and serve.

Nutritional Facts: (Per serving)

- ❖ Calories: 350
- ❖ Protein: 30g
- ❖ Fat: 25g
- ❖ Carbs: 3g

This roasted beef brisket flat steak combines convenience and gourmet taste in one dish, perfect for a cozy family dinner or meal prepping. Enjoy the succulent flavors and effortless cooking process, making every meal memorable and delicious.

Recipe 23: Swedish Meatballs

Get ready to indulge in Swedish meatballs' rich, savory flavors in a creamy sauce crafted perfectly for your Keto lifestyle. This recipe combines tender beef meatballs with a luscious, low-carb sauce, all prepared effortlessly in your Instant Pot. These meatballs will surely delight your taste buds and keep you on track with your Keto goals, perfect for a cozy dinner or a special occasion.

Servings: 4

Prepping Time: 15 minutes

Cook Time: 25 minutes

Difficulty: Moderate

Ingredients:

- 1 lb ground beef
- 1/4 cup almond flour
- 1/4 cup grated Parmesan cheese
- 1 egg
- 1/2 tsp salt
- 1/2 tsp black pepper
- 1/4 tsp nutmeg
- 1/4 cup heavy cream
- 1/4 cup beef broth
- 2 tbsp butter
- 1/2 cup sour cream
- 1/2 tsp Dijon mustard
- Fresh parsley for garnish (optional)

Step-by-Step Preparation:

1. Combine ground beef, almond flour, Parmesan cheese, egg, salt, pepper, and nutmeg in a large bowl. Mix until well combined.
2. Form the mixture into 1-inch meatballs.
3. Set the Instant Pot to saute mode and melt the butter.
4. Add the meatballs in batches, browning them on all sides. Remove and set aside.
5. Pour the beef broth into the pot, scraping any browned bits from the bottom.
6. Place the meatballs back into the pot, seal the lid, and set to high pressure for 7 minutes.
7. Once cooking is complete, perform a quick release.
8. Remove the meatballs and set the pot to saute mode.
9. Stir in the heavy cream, sour cream, and Dijon mustard, cooking until the sauce thickens.
10. Return the meatballs to the sauce, coating them evenly.
11. Garnish with fresh parsley before serving, if desired.

Nutritional Facts (Per serving)

- Calories: 350
- Protein: 25g
- Fat: 28g
- Carbohydrates: 4g
- Fiber: 1g

Savor the comforting taste of these Keto Swedish meatballs in a creamy sauce, a hearty and health-conscious dish. Whether sharing with family or enjoying a quiet night, this recipe will become a favorite. Enjoy the rich flavors and the ease of preparation, knowing you're staying true to your Keto journey.

Recipe 24: Beef Striploin Steak

Get ready to elevate your barbecue game with this delicious grilled beef barbecue striploin steak topped with zesty chimichurri sauce. Perfect for Keto enthusiasts, this Instant Pot recipe ensures juicy, tender beef every time, making it an irresistible main dish.

Servings: 4

Prepping Time: 15 minutes

Cook Time: 45 minutes

Difficulty: Medium

Ingredients:

- ✓ 4 striploin steaks
- ✓ 1/4 cup olive oil
- ✓ 2 tablespoons red wine vinegar
- ✓ 1/2 cup fresh parsley, chopped
- ✓ 3 cloves garlic, minced
- ✓ 1 teaspoon dried oregano
- ✓ 1/2 teaspoon red pepper flakes
- ✓ Salt and pepper to taste

Step-by-Step Preparation:

1. Prepare the Chimichurri Sauce: In a bowl, combine olive oil, red wine vinegar, parsley, garlic, oregano, red pepper flakes, salt, and pepper. Mix well and set aside.
2. Season the Steaks: Season the striploin steaks generously with salt and pepper on both sides.
3. Sear the Steaks: Set the Instant Pot to 'Saute' mode. Once hot, add the steaks and sear on each side for 2-3 minutes until browned.
4. Pressure Cook: Pour half of the chimichurri sauce over the steaks, then seal the Instant Pot lid. Cook on high pressure for 15 minutes.
5. Natural Release: Allow the pressure to release naturally for 10 minutes, then quickly release any remaining pressure.
6. Serve: Transfer the steaks to a plate, drizzle with the remaining chimichurri sauce, and serve immediately.

Nutritional Facts: (Per serving)

- ❖ Calories: 350
- ❖ Protein: 30g
- ❖ Fat: 25g
- ❖ Carbohydrates: 2g
- ❖ Fiber: 1g

Experience the robust flavors and simplicity of this grilled beef barbecue striploin steak with chimichurri sauce. Ideal for keto diets, this dish promises a deliciously satisfying meal, perfect for family dinners or special occasions. Enjoy the perfect balance of juicy steak and fresh, zesty sauce with minimal effort using your Instant Pot.

Recipe 25: Beef With Balsamic Vinegar

This mouthwatering Keto Instant Pot recipe features tender beef roasted with balsamic vinegar, crisp green beans, and peppery arugula. It's a perfect main dish for those on a keto diet, combining rich flavors and healthy ingredients for a satisfying meal.

Servings: 4

Cook Time: 45 minutes

Prepping Time: 15 minutes

Difficulty: Moderate

Ingredients:

- ✓ 1.5 lbs beef roast
- ✓ 1/4 cup balsamic vinegar
- ✓ 1 lb green beans, trimmed
- ✓ 2 cups arugula
- ✓ 2 tbsp olive oil
- ✓ 3 cloves garlic, minced
- ✓ Salt and pepper to taste

Step-by-Step Preparation:

1. Season the beef roast with salt and pepper.
2. Heat olive oil in the Instant Pot and sear the beef on all sides.
3. Add minced garlic and cook for 1 minute.
4. Pour in the balsamic vinegar, ensuring the meat is well-coated.
5. Seal the Instant Pot lid and cook on high pressure for 35 minutes.
6. Quickly release the pressure and add green beans.
7. Cook on high pressure for an additional 5 minutes.
8. Quick release, then remove the beef and green beans.
9. Slice the meat and serve with green beans and fresh arugula.

Nutritional Facts: (Per serving)

- ❖ Calories: 380
- ❖ Protein: 30g
- ❖ Fat: 25g
- ❖ Carbs: 5g
- ❖ Fiber: 2g

Enjoy this deliciously easy Keto Instant Pot beef roast with balsamic vinegar, green beans, and arugula. It's a hearty, low-carb meal perfect for dinner any night of the week. The combination of tender beef, tangy balsamic, and fresh greens will satisfy you and your family.

Recipe 26: Beef Stroganoff With Mushrooms

Beef Stroganoff with Mushrooms is a delectable, hearty dish perfect for a keto diet. This Instant Pot recipe ensures tender beef and a rich, creamy sauce infused with mushrooms, all in a fraction of the usual cooking time.

Servings: 4

Prepping Time: 15 minutes

Cook Time: 30 minutes

Difficulty: Medium

Ingredients:

- ✓ 1 lb beef sirloin, thinly sliced
- ✓ 1 cup mushrooms, sliced
- ✓ 1 small onion, chopped
- ✓ 2 cloves garlic, minced
- ✓ 1 cup beef broth
- ✓ 1 cup heavy cream
- ✓ 2 tbsp sour cream
- ✓ 2 tbsp olive oil
- ✓ Salt and pepper to taste
- ✓ 1 tsp paprika
- ✓ 1 tbsp fresh parsley, chopped (optional)

Step-by-Step Preparation:

1. Preheat your Instant Pot on the saute setting, and add olive oil.
2. Saute the onions and garlic until fragrant, about 3 minutes.
3. Add the beef slices, season with salt, pepper, and paprika, and cook until browned.
4. Stir in the mushrooms and cook for another 5 minutes.
5. Pour the beef broth, secure the lid, and set the Instant Pot to high pressure for 20 minutes.
6. Quickly release the pressure, then stir in the heavy and sour cream.
7. Simmer on the saute setting until the sauce thickens, about 5 minutes.
8. Garnish with fresh parsley before serving.

Nutritional Facts: (Per serving)

- ❖ **Calories:** 400
- ❖ **Protein:** 25g
- ❖ **Fat:** 30g
- ❖ **Carbohydrates:** 5g
- ❖ **Fiber:** 1g

Enjoy your Beef Stroganoff with Mushrooms, a satisfying meal that's low in carbs but high in flavor. Perfect for a cozy night in, this dish pairs wonderfully with zoodles or cauliflower rice, making it a versatile addition to your keto meal plan. Happy cooking.

Recipe 27: Spicy Meat Beef Curry

Craving a hearty meal that's low on carbs but high on flavor? Our Spicy Delicious Beef Curry is the perfect Keto Instant Pot recipe to satisfy your taste buds. This dish will become a favorite with bold spices and tender beef in no time. It's quick to prepare and packed with nutrients, making it ideal for any day of the week.

Servings: 4

Prepping Time: 15 minutes

Cook Time: 45 minutes

Difficulty: Medium

Ingredients:

- ✓ 1.5 lbs beef stew meat, cut into cubes
- ✓ 1 large onion, finely chopped
- ✓ 3 cloves garlic, minced
- ✓ 1-inch ginger, grated
- ✓ 2 tablespoons curry powder
- ✓ 1 teaspoon cumin
- ✓ 1 teaspoon paprika
- ✓ 1 teaspoon turmeric
- ✓ 1 teaspoon chili powder
- ✓ 1 can coconut milk (14 oz)
- ✓ 1 cup beef broth
- ✓ 2 tablespoons tomato paste
- ✓ 2 tablespoons olive oil
- ✓ Salt and pepper to taste
- ✓ Fresh cilantro for garnish

Step-by-Step Preparation:

1. Set the Instant Pot to saute mode and heat the olive oil.
2. Add the chopped onion, garlic, and ginger. Saute until fragrant.
3. Add the beef cubes and brown on all sides.
4. Stir in the curry powder, cumin, paprika, turmeric, and chili powder. Cook for 2 minutes.
5. Add the tomato paste and mix well.
6. Pour in the beef broth and coconut milk, stirring to combine.
7. Seal the Instant Pot lid and set it to pressure cook on high for 35 minutes.
8. Once done, release the pressure naturally for 10 minutes, then quickly release the remaining pressure.
9. Open the lid, season with salt and pepper, and garnish with fresh cilantro.

Nutritional Facts: (Per serving)

- ❖ Calories: 390
- ❖ Protein: 28g
- ❖ Fat: 28g
- ❖ Carbohydrates: 5g
- ❖ Fiber: 2g

Dive into a spicy, delicious beef curry bowl and experience a symphony of flavors. This keto-friendly dish pairs beautifully with cauliflower rice or a fresh green salad, perfect for a cozy dinner. Enjoy a satisfying meal that aligns with your dietary goals and leaves you full and happy.

Recipe 28: Beef Bourguignon

Beef Bourguignon Ragout with Carrots and Thyme is a delightful, hearty dish perfect for a cozy dinner. With tender beef and a rich, savory sauce, this keto-friendly recipe will impress. It's quick and easy to prepare using an Instant Pot, making it an excellent option for busy weeknights or special occasions.

Servings: 6

Prepping Time: 20 minutes

Cook Time: 1 hour

Difficulty: Medium

Ingredients:

- 2 lbs beef chuck, cubed
- 4 slices bacon, diced
- 1 onion, chopped
- 2 cloves garlic, minced
- 3 carrots, sliced
- 1 cup beef broth
- 1 cup red wine
- 1 tbsp tomato paste
- 1 tsp thyme
- 1 bay leaf
- Salt and pepper to taste

Step-by-Step Preparation:

1. Prepare the Beef: Season beef cubes with salt and pepper.
2. Saute the Bacon: Using the saute function on the Instant Pot, cook the bacon until crispy. Remove and set aside.
3. Brown the Beef: In the bacon fat, brown the beef cubes on all sides. Remove and set aside.
4. Cook the Aromatics: Add onion, garlic, and carrots to the pot. Saute until onions are translucent.
5. Combine Ingredients: Return beef and bacon to the pot. Add beef broth, red wine, tomato paste, thyme, and bay leaf. Stir well.
6. Pressure Cook: Seal the Instant Pot and cook on high pressure for 40 minutes. Let the pressure release naturally.
7. Serve: Remove bay leaf, stir, and serve hot.

Nutritional Facts: (Per serving)

- Calories: 450
- Fat: 25g
- Protein: 40g
- Carbohydrates: 10g
- Fiber: 3g

Enjoy your Beef Bourguignon Ragout with Carrots and Thyme as a comforting and nutritious meal. The Instant Pot ensures the beef is perfectly tender, and the flavors are deeply infused, making every bite a delight. This dish will quickly become a family favorite, perfect for a keto-friendly diet.

Recipe 29: Mexican Tacos With Meat

Craving something deliciously spicy yet keto-friendly? Our Mexican Tacos with Meat, Beans, and Salsa are here to satisfy your taste buds. With the ease of an Instant Pot, you'll whip up this savory main dish in no time. These tacos are a flavor-packed, low-carb delight for a quick weeknight dinner.

Servings: 4

Cook Time: 20 minutes

Prepping Time: 10 minutes

Difficulty: Medium

Ingredients:

- ✓ 1 lb ground beef
- ✓ 1 cup black beans (drained and rinsed)
- ✓ 1 cup salsa
- ✓ 1 tsp chili powder
- ✓ 1 tsp cumin
- ✓ 1/2 tsp garlic powder
- ✓ 1/2 tsp onion powder
- ✓ Salt and pepper to taste
- ✓ 1 tbsp olive oil
- ✓ Lettuce leaves or keto-friendly tortillas
- ✓ Optional toppings: shredded cheese, avocado, sour cream, cilantro

Step-by-Step Preparation:

1. Set the Instant Pot to saute mode and heat the olive oil.
2. Add the ground beef and cook until browned. Drain excess fat.
3. Stir in the chili powder, cumin, garlic powder, onion powder, salt, and pepper.
4. Add the black beans and salsa and mix well.
5. Close the lid and set it to manual high pressure for 10 minutes.
6. Once done, perform a quick release. Open the lid carefully.
7. Spoon the mixture onto lettuce leaves or keto-friendly tortillas.
8. Add your favorite toppings and serve hot.

Nutritional Facts: (Per serving)

- ❖ Calories: 320
- ❖ Protein: 25g
- ❖ Fat: 22g
- ❖ Carbohydrates: 8g
- ❖ Fiber: 4g
- ❖ Net Carbs: 4g

Enjoy these Mexican Tacos with Meat, Beans, and Salsa as a guilt-free keto delight. Perfect for busy nights, they're easy to make and flavorful. Whether you're a keto veteran or just starting out, this dish will become a new favorite in your meal rotation.

Recipe 30: Roasted Beef With Broccoli

Looking for a quick and delicious keto-friendly meal? Try our Roasted Beef with Broccoli Vegetables, made effortlessly in an Instant Pot. This main dish is perfect for busy weeknights when you need a nutritious and flavorful dinner on the table quickly.

Servings: 4

Prepping Time: 15 minutes

Cook Time: 30 minutes

Difficulty: Medium

Ingredients:

- ✓ 1 lb beef roast
- ✓ 2 cups broccoli florets
- ✓ 1 tbsp olive oil
- ✓ 1 tsp garlic powder
- ✓ 1 tsp onion powder
- ✓ Salt and pepper to taste
- ✓ 1 cup beef broth

Step-by-Step Preparation:

1. Prepare the Beef: Season the beef roast with garlic powder, onion powder, salt, and pepper.
2. Saute Mode: Set the Instant Pot to saute mode, add olive oil, and sear the beef on all sides.
3. Add Broth: Pour in the beef broth, submerging the meat partially.
4. Cook: Close the lid and set the Instant Pot to pressure cook on high for 25 minutes.
5. Add Broccoli: Quickly release the pressure, add broccoli florets, and cook for 5 minutes.
6. Serve: Let it naturally release pressure, then serve hot.

Nutritional Facts (Per serving)

- ❖ Calories: 250
- ❖ Protein: 25g
- ❖ Fat: 15g
- ❖ Carbohydrates: 5g
- ❖ Fiber: 2g

Enjoy a hearty and wholesome meal with our Roasted Beef and Broccoli. Perfect for your keto diet, it's packed with nutrients and bursting with flavor, ensuring you stay satisfied without compromising your health goals.

Chapter 4: Main Dishes Poultry

Recipe 31: Butter Chicken Curry

Butter chicken curry with basmati rice and limes is a delicious, keto-friendly dish perfect for any night of the week. The creamy, spiced curry pairs beautifully with fragrant basmati rice and a squeeze of fresh lime juice. Made effortlessly in an Instant Pot, this recipe saves time without compromising flavor.

Servings: 4

Prepping Time: 15 minutes

Cook Time: 30 minutes

Difficulty: Medium

Ingredients:

- 2 lbs boneless, skinless chicken thighs, cubed
- 1 cup full-fat coconut milk
- 1 cup tomato puree
- 1 large onion, finely chopped
- 3 cloves garlic, minced
- 1 tbsp ginger, grated
- 2 tbsp butter
- 1 tbsp garam masala
- 1 tsp turmeric powder
- 1 tsp chili powder
- 1 tsp cumin powder
- Salt to taste
- 1 cup basmati rice
- 2 cups water
- Fresh limes, quartered
- Fresh cilantro for garnish

Step-by-Step Preparation:

1. Set the Instant Pot to saute mode. Add butter, onions, garlic, and ginger. Saute until onions are translucent.
2. Add garam masala, turmeric, chili powder, and cumin powder. Stir well to combine.
3. Add cubed chicken thighs and cook until browned on all sides.
4. Pour in the tomato puree and coconut milk. Stir to mix.
5. Secure the lid on the Instant Pot and set it to high pressure for 10 minutes.
6. Meanwhile, rinse the basmati rice under cold water. Combine rice and water in a rice cooker or saucepan. Cook according to package instructions.
7. After the Instant Pot timer goes off, allow a natural release for 10 minutes before performing a quick release.
8. Serve the butter chicken over basmati rice, garnished with fresh cilantro and lime wedges.

Nutritional Facts: (Per serving)

- Calories: 450
- Protein: 35g
- Fat: 25g
- Carbohydrates: 20g
- Fiber: 3g

Enjoy the rich and flavorful experience of butter chicken curry with basmati rice. Perfect for a keto diet and prepared with ease in an Instant Pot, this dish is sure to become a favorite. It offers a delightful combination of spices and creamy textures that will leave everyone satisfied.

Recipe 32: Green Chicken Curry

Ready to indulge in a rich and flavorful dish without breaking your keto diet? This Green Chicken Curry, made effortlessly in an Instant Pot, is the perfect blend of aromatic spices and tender chicken. Ideal for busy weeknights or impressing guests, this dish will become a staple in your kitchen.

Servings: 4

Prepping Time: 15 minutes

Cook Time: 25 minutes

Difficulty: Medium

Ingredients:

- 1 lb boneless, skinless chicken thighs cut into chunks
- 2 tbsp coconut oil
- 1 onion, finely chopped
- 3 cloves garlic, minced
- 1-inch piece ginger, grated
- 2 tbsp green curry paste
- 1 can (13.5 oz) coconut milk
- 1 cup chicken broth
- 1 bell pepper, sliced
- 1 zucchini, sliced
- 1 cup spinach leaves
- 1 tbsp fish sauce
- 1 tsp lime juice
- Salt and pepper to taste
- Fresh cilantro for garnish

Step-by-Step Preparation:

1. Set the Instant Pot to saute mode and heat the coconut oil.
2. Add the chopped onion, garlic, and grated ginger. Saute until fragrant.
3. Stir in the green curry paste and cook for another minute.
4. Add the chicken chunks and cook until slightly browned.
5. Pour in the coconut milk and chicken broth, stirring well.
6. Add bell pepper, zucchini, and spinach leaves. Season with fish sauce, lime juice, salt, and pepper.
7. Seal the Instant Pot lid and set it to high pressure for 10 minutes.
8. Allow a natural pressure release for 10 minutes before a quick release.
9. Open the lid, stir the curry, and garnish with fresh cilantro.

Nutritional Facts: (Per serving)

- Calories: 350
- Fat: 28g
- Carbohydrates: 6g
- Fiber: 2g
- Protein: 20g

Enjoy this delightful Green Chicken Curry, which is both keto-friendly and bursting with flavor. It's a simple, quick dish that doesn't skimp on taste or nutrition. It's perfect for satisfying your cravings while keeping your diet on track. Serve it hot, and savor every bite.

Recipe 33: Alfredo Pasta With Chicken

Indulge in the rich and creamy flavors of our Keto Alfredo Pasta with Chicken, Mushrooms, and Parmesan Cheese, made effortlessly in your Instant Pot. This dish combines tender chicken with savory mushrooms and a luscious Alfredo sauce, perfect for a low-carb, high-fat diet. Quick to prepare and flavorful, this recipe will be a new favorite in your keto meal rotation.

Servings: 4

Prepping Time: 10 minutes

Cook Time: 20 minutes

Difficulty: Easy

Ingredients:
- 2 tablespoons butter
- 2 boneless, skinless chicken breasts, diced
- 1 cup sliced mushrooms
- 2 cloves garlic, minced
- 1 cup heavy cream
- 1 cup grated Parmesan cheese
- 1 cup chicken broth
- 1 teaspoon Italian seasoning
- Salt and pepper to taste
- 1 package of keto-friendly pasta (such as shirataki noodles)

Step-by-Step Preparation:
1. Set your Instant Pot to saute mode and melt the butter.
2. Add the diced chicken and cook until browned.
3. Add the mushrooms and garlic, sauteing for 2-3 minutes.
4. Pour in the chicken broth, heavy cream, and Italian seasoning. Stir well.
5. Add the Parmesan cheese, mixing until thoroughly melted and combined.
6. Add the keto-friendly pasta, ensuring it is well coated in the sauce.
7. Close the Instant Pot lid, set to high pressure, and cook for 5 minutes.
8. Quickly release the pressure, stir the pasta, and season with salt and pepper to taste.

Nutritional Facts: (Per serving)
- Calories: 450
- Fat: 35g
- Protein: 25g
- Carbs: 6g
- Fiber: 2g

Enjoy the creamy decadence of this Keto Alfredo Pasta with Chicken, Mushrooms, and Parmesan Cheese. It's perfect for a satisfying weeknight dinner that aligns with your low-carb lifestyle. Whether you're a seasoned keto follower or new to the diet, this dish will become a staple in your kitchen, delivering rich flavors without the guilt.

Recipe 34: Chicken Tikka With Rice

Chicken Tikka Masala with Rice is a flavorful and aromatic dish that perfectly fits your keto diet. This Instant Pot recipe allows you to enjoy a rich, creamy sauce with tender chicken pieces over a bed of cauliflower rice. It's quick to make and brings the exotic taste of Indian cuisine right to your kitchen.

Servings: 4

Cook Time: 30 minutes

Prepping Time: 15 minutes

Difficulty: Medium

Ingredients:

- 1 lb boneless, skinless chicken thighs, cubed
- 1 cup heavy cream
- 1 cup tomato sauce
- 2 tbsp ghee or butter
- 1 onion, finely chopped
- 3 cloves garlic, minced
- 1 tbsp ginger, minced
- 2 tbsp garam masala
- 1 tsp turmeric
- 1 tsp cumin
- 1 tsp paprika
- 1 tsp chili powder
- 1/2 tsp salt
- 1/2 cup fresh cilantro, chopped
- 2 cups cauliflower rice

Step-by-Step Preparation:

1. Set the Instant Pot to saute mode and melt the ghee or butter.
2. Add the chopped onion, garlic, and ginger. Saute until fragrant.
3. Add the garam masala, turmeric, cumin, paprika, chili powder, and salt. Stir well.
4. Add the cubed chicken and cook until lightly browned on all sides.
5. Pour in the tomato sauce and heavy cream. Stir to combine.
6. Close the Instant Pot lid and set it to high pressure for 15 minutes.
7. Quickly release the pressure, then stir in the chopped cilantro.
8. Serve over cauliflower rice.

Nutritional Facts: (Per serving)

- Calories: 350
- Protein: 25g
- Fat: 25g
- Carbohydrates: 8g
- Fiber: 3g

Enjoy this delicious Chicken Tikka Masala with Rice, which caters to your keto lifestyle while satisfying your taste buds. The Instant Pot makes it easy to prepare, ensuring a hassle-free cooking experience. Treat yourself and your family to this nutritious, indulgent, wholesome meal.

Recipe 35: Buffalo Wings With Dip

Craving a game-day classic? These Spicy Homemade Buffalo Wings with Dip and Beer are your answer. Perfect for keto enthusiasts, this Instant Pot recipe delivers tender, juicy wings with a fiery kick, all in under an hour. Whether entertaining friends or enjoying a cozy night, these wings are a sure hit.

Servings: 4

Prepping Time: 15 minutes

Cook Time: 30 minutes

Difficulty: Medium

Ingredients:

- ✓ 2 lbs chicken wings
- ✓ 1/2 cup hot sauce
- ✓ 1/4 cup butter
- ✓ 1 tbsp apple cider vinegar
- ✓ 1 tsp garlic powder
- ✓ 1 tsp onion powder
- ✓ Salt and pepper to taste
- ✓ Blue cheese or ranch dip
- ✓ Your favorite low-carb beer

Step-by-Step Preparation:

1. Season the chicken wings with salt, pepper, garlic powder, and onion powder.
2. Place the wings in the Instant Pot with 1/2 cup of water.
3. Cook on high pressure for 10 minutes, then release the pressure manually.
4. In a small saucepan, melt the butter and mix in the hot sauce and vinegar.
5. Preheat your oven to broil.
6. Toss the cooked wings in the hot sauce mixture and place them on a baking sheet.
7. Broil for 5-7 minutes until crispy.
8. Serve hot with dip and beer.

Nutritional Facts (Per serving)

- ❖ Calories: 320
- ❖ Protein: 28g
- ❖ Fat: 22g
- ❖ Carbs: 2g
- ❖ Fiber: 0g

Looking for the ultimate wing experience? These keto-friendly buffalo wings, paired with a creamy dip and refreshing beer, promise to satisfy your spicy cravings. Quick and easy with the Instant Pot, they're perfect for any occasion. Enjoy every mouthwatering bite.

Recipe 36: Chili Chicken With Chives

Craving a spicy, savory dish that fits your keto lifestyle? Look no further than Chili Chicken Garnished with Garlic Chives. This Instant Pot recipe is quick, easy, and flavorful, perfect for busy weeknights. Prepare to enjoy a delicious meal that will leave your taste buds tingling.

Servings: 4

Prepping Time: 10 minutes

Cook Time: 20 minutes

Difficulty: Easy

Ingredients:

- 1 lb boneless, skinless chicken thighs
- 1 cup chicken broth
- 2 tbsp olive oil
- 1 tbsp soy sauce
- 2 tsp chili powder
- 1 tsp garlic powder
- 1 tsp onion powder
- Salt and pepper to taste
- 1/4 cup chopped garlic chives

Step-by-Step Preparation:

1. Set the Instant Pot to saute mode and add olive oil.
2. Season chicken thighs with salt, pepper, garlic powder, and onion powder.
3. Brown the chicken thighs on both sides in the Instant Pot.
4. Add chicken broth, soy sauce, and chili powder.
5. Secure the lid and set the Instant Pot to pressure cook on high for 10 minutes.
6. Once done, let the pressure release naturally for 10 minutes, then quickly release any remaining pressure.
7. Remove the lid and garnish with chopped garlic chives before serving.

Nutritional Facts: (Per serving)

- Calories: 250
- Protein: 25g
- Fat: 15g
- Carbohydrates: 2g
- Fiber: 0g
- Sugar: 0g

Ready to spice up your keto meal plan? This chili chicken, garnished with garlic chives, is easy and incredibly satisfying. Enjoy this delicious dish as part of your healthy eating routine and savor every bite.

Recipe 37: Chicken With Teriyaki Sauce

Savor the delightful flavors of Grilled Chicken with Teriyaki Sauce, a perfect main dish for your keto diet. This quick and easy recipe prepared using an Instant Pot, offers a juicy and flavorful meal that's sure to impress. Whether you're new to keto or a seasoned pro, this dish is a crowd-pleaser.

Servings: 4

Prepping Time: 10 minutes

Cook Time: 20 minutes

Difficulty: Easy

Ingredients:

- 4 boneless, skinless chicken breasts
- 1/2 cup soy sauce
- 1/4 cup water
- 2 tablespoons apple cider vinegar
- 2 tablespoons granulated erythritol
- 1 teaspoon garlic powder
- 1 teaspoon ground ginger
- 1/4 teaspoon black pepper
- 1 tablespoon sesame oil
- 2 tablespoons olive oil

Step-by-Step Preparation:

1. Mix soy sauce, water, apple cider vinegar, erythritol, garlic powder, ginger, black pepper, and sesame oil in a bowl.
2. Pour the mixture into the Instant Pot and add the chicken breasts.
3. Set the Instant Pot to "Pressure Cook" on high for 15 minutes.
4. Once done, allow the pressure to release naturally for 5 minutes, then quickly release any remaining pressure.
5. Remove the chicken and set aside. Switch the Instant Pot to "Saute" and reduce the sauce until thickened.
6. Brush the chicken with olive oil and grill on a preheated grill for 2-3 minutes per side.
7. Serve the grilled chicken with the thickened teriyaki sauce drizzled on top.

Nutritional Facts (Per serving)

- Calories: 250
- Protein: 30g
- Fat: 12g
- Carbohydrates: 3g
- Fiber: 0g

Enjoy the perfect balance of sweet and savory with this keto-friendly Grilled Chicken with Teriyaki Sauce. It's a simple yet delicious dish that pairs well with steamed vegetables or a fresh salad. Make this recipe a staple in your keto meal rotation and delight your taste buds with every bite.

Recipe 38: Chicken With Potatoes

For a delightful dinner that combines the tangy taste of lemon with the savory flavor of garlic, try this Keto Lemon Garlic Chicken with Roasted Potatoes, Spices, and Herbs. It's a simple yet delicious dish perfect for any night of the week, made easy with an Instant Pot.

Servings: 4

Prepping Time: 15 minutes

Cook Time: 30 minutes

Difficulty: Easy

Ingredients:

- 4 boneless, skinless chicken breasts
- 2 tablespoons olive oil
- 1 lemon, juiced and zested
- 4 cloves garlic, minced
- 1 teaspoon dried thyme
- 1 teaspoon dried rosemary
- 1 teaspoon paprika
- Salt and pepper to taste
- 1 pound baby potatoes, halved
- 1 cup chicken broth

Step-by-Step Preparation:

1. Turn on the Instant Pot and select the saute function. Add olive oil.
2. Season chicken breasts with salt, pepper, paprika, thyme, and rosemary.
3. Saute chicken for 3-4 minutes on each side until browned. Remove and set aside.
4. Add minced garlic to the pot and saute for 1 minute.
5. Pour in chicken broth, lemon juice, and zest, scraping up any browned bits.
6. Return chicken to the pot and add potatoes on top.
7. Seal the Instant Pot and cook on high pressure for 15 minutes.
8. Quickly release the pressure, remove the lid, and serve.

Nutritional Facts: (Per serving)

- Calories: 320
- Protein: 35g
- Fat: 15g
- Carbohydrates: 10g
- Fiber: 3g

This Keto Lemon Garlic Chicken with Roasted Potatoes is a surefire hit for anyone looking for a healthy, flavorful meal. The zesty lemon and aromatic herbs make each bite irresistible. Enjoy this quick and easy dish, perfect for a busy weeknight dinner.

Recipe 39: Chicken Cacciatore

Chicken Cacciatore is a classic Italian dish perfect for a keto diet, thanks to its low-carb ingredients and rich flavors. Made easily in an Instant Pot, this recipe is a weeknight savior, bringing comfort and convenience to your dinner table. The combination of tender chicken, vibrant vegetables, and savory herbs makes it a crowd-pleaser.

Servings: 4

Prepping Time: 10 minutes

Cook Time: 30 minutes

Difficulty: Medium

Ingredients:

- 4 boneless, skinless chicken thighs
- 1 bell pepper, sliced
- 1 onion, chopped
- 2 cloves garlic, minced
- 1 can diced tomatoes (14.5 oz)
- 1/2 cup chicken broth
- 1/4 cup dry white wine
- 1 tsp dried oregano
- 1 tsp dried basil
- 1/2 tsp salt
- 1/4 tsp black pepper
- 2 tbsp olive oil

Step-by-Step Preparation:

1. Set the Instant Pot to saute mode and heat the olive oil.
2. Add chicken thighs and brown on both sides. Remove and set aside.
3. Saute bell pepper, onion, and garlic in the Instant Pot until softened.
4. Pour in the wine, scraping up any browned bits.
5. Add the diced tomatoes, chicken broth, oregano, basil, salt, and pepper. Stir well.
6. Return the chicken to the pot, submerging it in the sauce.
7. Close the lid and set it to high pressure for 15 minutes. Let the pressure release naturally for 10 minutes.
8. Open the lid, remove the chicken, and set the pot to saute mode to thicken the sauce for 5 minutes.
9. Serve the chicken topped with the sauce.

Nutritional Facts: (Per serving)

- Calories: 280
- Protein: 25g
- Fat: 18g
- Carbohydrates: 6g
- Fiber: 2g

Chicken cacciatore is a delightful and healthy meal for those following a keto lifestyle. Thanks to the Instant Pot, this dish requires minimal prep and cooking time and quickly brings robust Italian flavors to your table. Enjoy a delicious, low-carb dinner that will become a favorite in your household.

Recipe 40: Chicken With Mashed Potatoes

Chicken Marsala with mashed potatoes and vegetables is a delightful Keto Instant Pot dish for any poultry lover. This recipe balances rich flavors and wholesome ingredients, making it an ideal main dish for a hearty meal. Whether new to cooking or a seasoned chef, this recipe's simplicity and taste will impress.

Servings: 4

Prepping Time: 15 minutes

Cook Time: 30 minutes

Difficulty: Easy

Ingredients:

- 4 boneless, skinless chicken breasts
- 1 cup marsala wine
- 1 cup chicken broth
- 1/2 cup heavy cream
- 1/4 cup olive oil
- 1 pound mashed potatoes (Keto-friendly)
- 2 cups mixed vegetables (broccoli, carrots, and zucchini)
- 1 onion, finely chopped
- 3 cloves garlic, minced
- Salt and pepper to taste
- Fresh parsley for garnish

Step-by-Step Preparation:

1. Set the Instant Pot to saute mode and heat olive oil.
2. Season the chicken breasts with salt and pepper.
3. Sear the chicken breasts in the Instant Pot until golden brown on both sides. Remove and set aside.
4. Add chopped onion and minced garlic to the pot and saute until translucent.
5. Pour in the marsala wine, scraping the bottom to deglaze the pot.
6. Add chicken broth and heavy cream, stirring to combine.
7. Return the chicken breasts to the pot, submerging them in the sauce.
8. Lock the lid and set the Instant Pot to pressure cook on high for 10 minutes.
9. Prepare the mashed potatoes and vegetables while the chicken cooks.
10. Release the pressure and remove the lid carefully.
11. Serve the chicken marsala over mashed potatoes with a side of mixed vegetables.
12. Garnish with fresh parsley and enjoy.

Nutritional Facts: (Per serving)

- Calories: 450
- Protein: 30g
- Fat: 25g
- Carbohydrates: 10g
- Fiber: 3g

Enjoy a burst of Italian flavors with this Chicken Marsala dish, paired perfectly with creamy mashed potatoes and a mix of fresh vegetables. It's an easy, quick, and nutritious meal that fits perfectly into your Keto diet.

Chapter 5: Main Dishes Seafood

Recipe 41: Lobster Tails With Butter Sauce

Indulge in a gourmet experience with our Seasoned Baked Lobster Tails with Lemon and Butter Sauce. This Keto-friendly recipe is perfect for a special occasion or a luxurious weeknight dinner. Succulent lobster tails are seasoned to perfection and paired with a rich, zesty sauce that will leave your taste buds craving more. Prepare to impress with this quick and easy Instant Pot dish.

Servings: 4

Cook Time: 10 minutes

Prepping Time: 15 minutes

Difficulty: Medium

Ingredients:

- 4 lobster tails
- 4 tablespoons unsalted butter, melted
- 2 cloves garlic, minced
- 1 lemon, juiced
- 1 teaspoon paprika
- 1 teaspoon sea salt
- 1/2 teaspoon black pepper
- 1/4 teaspoon cayenne pepper (optional)
- Fresh parsley, chopped (for garnish)

Step-by-Step Preparation:

1. Preheat your oven to 425°F (220°C).
2. Butterfly the lobster tails by cutting down the middle of the shells and pulling the meat out slightly.
3. Mix melted butter, garlic, lemon juice, paprika, salt, pepper, and cayenne pepper in a small bowl.
4. Brush the lobster tails with the butter mixture, ensuring even coverage.
5. Place the lobster tails in the Instant Pot and cook on high pressure for 3 minutes.
6. Carefully release the pressure and transfer the lobster tails to a baking sheet.
7. Bake in the oven for 5-7 minutes until the lobster meat is opaque and cooked.
8. Garnish with fresh parsley and serve immediately.

Nutritional Facts: (Per serving)

- Calories: 230
- Protein: 20g
- Fat: 16g
- Carbohydrates: 2g
- Fiber: 0g
- Sugar: 0g

Savor the exquisite flavors of these perfectly seasoned lobster tails, ideal for those following a keto diet. The Instant Pot makes preparation a breeze, while the oven finish ensures a tender, flavorful result. Whether you're hosting a dinner party or treating yourself to something special, this dish is sure to impress and satisfy. Enjoy your culinary masterpiece.

Recipe 42: Shrimp Scampi With Garlic

Sprinkled with parsley, shrimp scampi with garlic and butter sauce is a delectable keto-friendly seafood dish perfect for an instant pot. This main dish is quick and easy and bursting with flavor, making it an excellent choice for a weeknight dinner.

Servings: 4

Prepping Time: 10 minutes

Cook Time: 15 minutes

Difficulty: Easy

Ingredients:

- 1 pound large shrimp, peeled and deveined
- 4 tablespoons butter
- 4 cloves garlic, minced
- 1/2 cup chicken broth
- 1/4 cup lemon juice
- 1/4 cup fresh parsley, chopped
- Salt and pepper to taste

Step-by-Step Preparation:

1. Set the Instant Pot to saute mode and melt the butter.
2. Add the garlic and cook until fragrant, about 1 minute.
3. Pour in the chicken broth and lemon juice, then simmer.
4. Add the shrimp, stirring to coat them in the sauce.
5. Close the lid and cook on high pressure for 3 minutes.
6. Quickly release the pressure and open the lid.
7. Stir in the chopped parsley, then season with salt and pepper to taste.
8. Serve hot, garnished with extra parsley if desired.

Nutritional Facts (Per serving)

- Calories: 210
- Protein: 18g
- Fat: 14g
- Carbohydrates: 3g
- Fiber: 1g

This shrimp scampi is a delightful and satisfying keto dish that pairs well with zoodles or a fresh green salad. It's a quick and flavorful meal perfect for any seafood lover looking to maintain a low-carb diet. Happy cooking.

Recipe 43: Salmon and Green Asparagus

Baked salmon, green asparagus with aromatic herbs, and lemon is a delightful, keto-friendly seafood recipe perfect for any occasion. Combining fresh salmon and tender asparagus with zesty lemon and fragrant spices, this dish is as nutritious as it is delicious.

Servings: 4

Prepping Time: 10 minutes

Cook Time: 20 minutes

Difficulty: Easy

Ingredients:
- 4 salmon fillets
- 1 lb green asparagus
- 2 lemons, sliced
- 2 tbsp olive oil
- 2 garlic cloves, minced
- 1 tsp dried thyme
- 1 tsp dried rosemary
- Salt and pepper to taste

Step-by-Step Preparation:
1. Preheat your Instant Pot to the saute setting.
2. Drizzle olive oil and saute minced garlic until fragrant.
3. Add salmon fillets and asparagus to the pot.
4. Season with thyme, rosemary, salt, and pepper.
5. Layer lemon slices over the salmon and asparagus.
6. Secure the lid and cook on high pressure for 7 minutes.
7. Quick-release the pressure and serve hot.

Nutritional Facts (Per serving)
- Calories: 350
- Protein: 30g
- Fat: 22g
- Carbs: 5g
- Fiber: 2g

Enjoy this easy-to-make, flavorful dish, perfect for a healthy keto diet. The combination of salmon and asparagus with a hint of lemon and herbs will make your taste buds dance.

Recipe 44: Tuna Steak Fish and Salad

Dive into a world of flavors with this Hot Spicy Tuna Steak and Green Leaf Salad, a perfect dish for those on a keto journey. Bursting with spices and paired with a fresh salad, this recipe is a breeze to whip up in your Instant Pot. Enjoy a meal that's as nutritious as it is delicious.

Servings: 4

Prepping Time: 15 minutes

Cook Time: 10 minutes

Difficulty: Medium

Ingredients:

- 4 tuna steaks
- 2 tablespoons olive oil
- 1 tablespoon chili powder
- 1 teaspoon paprika
- 1 teaspoon garlic powder
- 1 teaspoon onion powder
- 1/2 teaspoon cayenne pepper
- Salt and pepper to taste
- 6 cups mixed green leaf salad
- 1 avocado, sliced
- 1 cucumber, sliced
- 1/4 cup olive oil (for dressing)
- 2 tablespoons lemon juice
- Salt and pepper to taste (for dressing)

Step-by-Step Preparation:

1. Mix chili powder, paprika, garlic powder, onion powder, cayenne pepper, salt, and pepper in a small bowl.
2. Rub the spice mixture onto the tuna steaks.
3. Set your Instant Pot to saute mode and add olive oil.
4. Sear the tuna steaks for 1-2 minutes on each side.
5. Switch the Instant Pot to pressure cook on high for 3 minutes.
6. While the tuna cooks, prepare the salad by tossing mixed greens, avocado, and cucumber.
7. Whisk together olive oil, lemon juice, salt, and pepper for the dressing.
8. Once the tuna is done, let it rest for a few minutes before serving.
9. Plate the tuna steaks with the salad and drizzle with the dressing.

Nutritional Facts: (Per serving)

- Calories: 320
- Protein: 35g
- Fat: 20g
- Carbohydrates: 4g
- Fiber: 3g

Enjoy this spicy, succulent tuna steak alongside a refreshing green salad for a balanced, keto-friendly meal. It's quick, easy, and packed with nutrients, making it a perfect choice for a healthy dinner.

Recipe 45: Cod With Beans and Potatoes

Get ready to tantalize your taste buds with our Tomato & Basil Chargrilled Cod with Green Beans and Potatoes. This keto-friendly dish, prepared effortlessly in an Instant Pot, offers a delightful combination of tender cod, fresh vegetables, and aromatic basil. Perfect for a quick yet gourmet meal, it's sure to become a favorite in your household.

Servings: 4

Prepping Time: 10 minutes

Cook Time: 15 minutes

Difficulty: Medium

Ingredients:
- 4 cod fillets
- 2 cups cherry tomatoes, halved
- 1 cup fresh basil leaves, chopped
- 2 cups green beans, trimmed
- 2 cups baby potatoes, halved
- 3 cloves garlic, minced
- 2 tablespoons olive oil
- Salt and pepper to taste
- Lemon wedges for garnish

Step-by-Step Preparation:
1. Season cod fillets with salt, pepper, and half the chopped basil.
2. Set the Instant Pot to saute mode and heat olive oil. Add garlic and cook until fragrant.
3. Add cherry tomatoes, green beans, and baby potatoes to the pot, stirring well.
4. Place cod fillets on top of the vegetables.
5. Secure the lid, set the Instant Pot to manual high pressure, and cook for 5 minutes.
6. Quick-release the pressure, open the lid, and carefully remove the cod.
7. Garnish with remaining basil and lemon wedges before serving.

Nutritional Facts: (Per serving)
- Calories: 300
- Protein: 25g
- Carbs: 15g
- Fat: 15g
- Fiber: 5g
- Net Carbs: 10g

Enjoy the fresh flavors of this Tomato & Basil Chargrilled Cod, a healthy and satisfying meal perfect for any day of the week. It's an excellent addition to your keto recipe collection, quick to make, and bursting with nutrients. Bon appetit.

Recipe 46: Shrimp Gumbo Prawns

Dive into the flavors of the South with this Keto Instant Pot Shrimp Gumbo Prawns in Spicy Tomato Sauce. This dish is perfect for any seafood lover on a keto diet, with a delightful blend of fresh shrimp, savory spices, and rich tomato sauce. Enjoy a hearty and nutritious meal that's easy to prepare and flavorful.

Servings: 4

Prepping Time: 15 minutes

Cook Time: 30 minutes

Difficulty: Medium

Ingredients:

- 1 lb shrimp, peeled and deveined
- 1 can (14.5 oz) diced tomatoes
- 1 medium onion, chopped
- 2 cloves garlic, minced
- 1 green bell pepper, chopped
- 1 cup chicken broth
- 2 tbsp olive oil
- 1 tsp smoked paprika
- 1/2 tsp cayenne pepper
- 1/2 tsp dried thyme
- Salt and pepper to taste
- 1 tbsp fresh parsley, chopped (for garnish)

Step-by-Step Preparation:

1. Prep the Instant Pot: Set the Instant Pot to saute mode and add olive oil.
2. Saute Vegetables: Add chopped onion, garlic, and bell pepper. Cook until soft.
3. Add Spices: Stir in smoked paprika, cayenne pepper, thyme, salt, and pepper.
4. Combine Ingredients: Add diced tomatoes, chicken broth, and shrimp. Stir well.
5. Cook: Secure the lid, set the Instant Pot to high pressure, and cook for 5 minutes.
6. Release Pressure: Use the quick-release method to release pressure.
7. Serve: Ladle the gumbo into bowls, garnish with fresh parsley, and enjoy.

Nutritional Facts: (Per serving)

- **Calories:** 210
- **Protein:** 25g
- **Fat:** 10g
- **Carbohydrates:** 5g
- **Fiber:** 2g
- **Net Carbs:** 3g

Treat yourself to this Keto Shrimp Gumbo Prawns in Spicy Tomato Sauce, a satisfying and nutritious meal that fits perfectly into your keto lifestyle. With its bold flavors and easy preparation, this dish will become a favorite in your household. Enjoy gumbo's comforting taste while staying on track with your health goals.

Recipe 47: Coconut Curry With Shrimps

Discover the exotic flavors of this Keto Instant Pot Coconut Curry with Shrimps, Chili, and Coriander. This delightful seafood dish is quick to prepare and perfect for a healthy, low-carb diet.

Servings: 4

Prepping Time: 15 minutes

Cook Time: 20 minutes

Difficulty: Medium

Ingredients:

- 1 lb shrimp, peeled and deveined
- 1 can of coconut milk
- 1 red chili, sliced
- 1 tbsp curry powder
- 1 tbsp coconut oil
- 1 onion, finely chopped
- 2 garlic cloves, minced
- 1-inch piece ginger, grated
- 1 tbsp fish sauce
- 1 lime, juiced
- Fresh coriander, chopped
- Salt and pepper to taste

Step-by-Step Preparation:

1. Set the Instant Pot to saute mode and heat the coconut oil.
2. Add the onion, garlic, and ginger, and saute until fragrant.
3. Stir in the curry powder and cook for another minute.
4. Add the shrimp, coconut milk, chili, and fish sauce.
5. Close the lid and set the Instant Pot to pressure cook on high for 5 minutes.
6. Release the pressure, stir in lime juice, and season with salt and pepper.
7. Garnish with fresh coriander before serving.

Nutritional Facts (Per serving)

- Calories: 250
- Protein: 25g
- Fat: 15g
- Carbohydrates: 5g
- Fiber: 2g

Enjoy this coconut curry's vibrant and creamy taste, a perfect blend of spice and freshness. This dish is ideal for busy weeknights, satisfying and nutritious, making it a staple for any keto seafood lover.

Recipe 48: Clam Chowder

Rich and creamy, this Keto Instant Pot Clam Chowder brings a taste of the sea to your table in no time. This low-carb version of the classic dish is both satisfying and nutritious, perfect for a cozy night in. With its easy preparation and delicious flavor, it's sure to become a favorite in your household.

Servings: 4

Prepping Time: 15 minutes

Cook Time: 20 minutes

Difficulty: Easy

Ingredients:
- 2 cups of chopped clams
- 1 cup of clam juice
- 1 cup of heavy cream
- 1/2 cup of diced celery
- 1/2 cup of diced onions
- 1/4 cup of butter
- 2 cloves of garlic, minced
- 1/2 teaspoon of dried thyme
- Salt and pepper to taste

Step-by-Step Preparation:
1. Set your Instant Pot to saute mode. Melt the butter and add the diced onions, celery, and garlic. Cook until the onions are translucent.
2. Stir in the chopped clams and juice. Cook for about 2 minutes.
3. Add the thyme, salt, and pepper. Secure the lid and set the Instant Pot to high pressure for 5 minutes.
4. Once the cooking cycle is complete, do a quick release. Stir in the heavy cream.
5. Switch the Instant Pot to saute mode again and let the chowder simmer for another 5 minutes to thicken.
6. Ladle the chowder into bowls and enjoy.

Nutritional Facts: (Per serving)
- Calories: 320
- Protein: 15g
- Fat: 28g
- Carbohydrates: 4g
- Fiber: 1g

This Keto Instant Pot Clam Chowder is a delightful meal that's easy to prepare and perfect for those following a low-carb diet. The Instant Pot ensures you can enjoy a hearty and flavorful dish quickly, making it an excellent addition to your weeknight dinner rotation. Enjoy the rich, comforting flavors of this seafood classic without the guilt.

Recipe 49: Mussels With Sauce

Baked green mussels with garlic butter herb sauce is a delightful keto-friendly seafood dish for any occasion. This Instant Pot recipe combines tender green mussels with a rich, flavorful garlic butter herb sauce, ensuring a mouthwatering experience. Whether new to seafood or a seasoned cook, this dish will impress your taste buds and guests.

Servings: 4

Prepping Time: 10 minutes

Cook Time: 15 minutes

Difficulty: Medium

Ingredients:

- ✓ 1 pound green mussels, cleaned
- ✓ 4 tablespoons unsalted butter
- ✓ 4 garlic cloves, minced
- ✓ 2 tablespoons fresh parsley, chopped
- ✓ 1 tablespoon fresh thyme, chopped
- ✓ Salt and pepper to taste
- ✓ Lemon wedges for serving

Step-by-Step Preparation:

1. Preheat the Instant Pot to saute mode and melt the butter.
2. Add the minced garlic and saute until fragrant, about 1 minute.
3. Stir in the parsley, thyme, salt, and pepper.
4. Place the mussels in the Instant Pot, ensuring they're well coated with the butter sauce.
5. Seal the Instant Pot and cook on high pressure for 5 minutes.
6. Quickly release the pressure and carefully open the lid.
7. Transfer the mussels to a serving platter, pouring any remaining sauce.
8. Serve with lemon wedges on the side.

Nutritional Facts: (Per serving)

- ❖ Calories: 180
- ❖ Protein: 18g
- ❖ Fat: 12g
- ❖ Carbohydrates: 2g
- ❖ Fiber: 0g

Enjoy this savory seafood dish that's both delicious and healthy. Perfect for keto enthusiasts, it delivers a satisfying meal without compromising flavor. Easy to prepare and quick to cook, these baked green mussels with garlic butter herb sauce will become a favorite in your recipe collection. Serve it up and watch your guests savor every bite.

Recipe 50: Grilled Scallops Shell

Indulge in the rich, savory flavors of grilled scallops shell with butter and garlic, a perfect keto-friendly main dish. This quick and easy recipe brings out scallops' natural sweetness, complemented by a luscious garlic butter sauce. Whether hosting a dinner party or enjoying a quiet night in, this seafood delight will impress your taste buds and guests.

Servings: 4

Prepping Time: 10 minutes

Cook Time: 15 minutes

Difficulty: Easy

Ingredients:

- ✓ 12 large scallops in the shell
- ✓ 4 tablespoons unsalted butter, melted
- ✓ 4 garlic cloves, minced
- ✓ 2 tablespoons fresh parsley, chopped
- ✓ 1 tablespoon lemon juice
- ✓ Salt and pepper to taste

Step-by-Step Preparation:

1. Preheat your grill to medium-high heat.
2. Rinse the scallops and pat them dry with paper towels.
3. Mix melted butter, minced garlic, parsley, lemon juice, salt, and pepper in a small bowl.
4. Place each scallop back in its shell and drizzle with the garlic butter mixture.
5. Grill the scallops in their shells for 5-7 minutes until they are opaque and slightly charred.
6. Remove from the grill and let them rest for a few minutes before serving.

Nutritional Facts: (Per serving)

- ❖ Calories: 180
- ❖ Protein: 18g
- ❖ Fat: 12g
- ❖ Carbohydrates: 2g
- ❖ Fiber: 0g
- ❖ Sugar: 0g

Serve these grilled scallop shells with butter and garlic as a standout dish for your next meal. The combination of tender scallops and rich, buttery garlic sauce creates a mouthwatering experience that's both keto-friendly and gourmet. This recipe will become a favorite in your seafood repertoire, perfect for any occasion.

Conclusion

Thank you for exploring the Simple Keto Instant Pot Cookbook: Healthy and Authentic Recipes With Stunning Photos by James A. Mabe. This cookbook is more than just a collection of recipes; it's a gateway to a healthier lifestyle, proving that you can enjoy delicious, nutritious meals without spending hours in the kitchen. Each recipe is designed to be easy, quick, and mouthwateringly good, making it a perfect addition to your keto journey.

From hearty breakfasts to savory dinners, this cookbook offers a wide range of dishes that cater to every meal of the day. The stunning photos make the recipes more appealing and guide you through the cooking process, ensuring that every dish turns out perfectly. James A. Mabe's attention to detail and dedication to creating authentic, keto-friendly recipes shine through on every page, making this cookbook a valuable resource for anyone looking to maintain a healthy lifestyle without compromising taste.

As you continue to explore these recipes, you'll discover new favorites that will become staples in your kitchen. The convenience of the Instant Pot combined with the benefits of a keto diet creates a winning formula that simplifies your cooking routine while enhancing your overall health and well-being.

We hope this cookbook inspires you to experiment with new ingredients, try different cooking techniques, and, most importantly, enjoy making delicious, healthy meals. Thank you for choosing the Simple Keto Instant Pot Cookbook.